Missing Links

December 9, 2017. Also called 'Weird Relationships'

COMBINED WITH: 'Module: Correlations'

Updated 2024

*Dedicated to my Dad, Michael J. Coppedge,
who helped inspire my work on correlations.*

CORRELATIONS AND MISSING LINKS

By NATHAN COPPEDGE

'''

KEY WORK*[1]: A WORK ON OPTICAL ILLUSIONS

LOGICAL BINARY OPPOSITE PHENOMENA

COHERENT-MAGIC

The way where M.C. Escher seems like magic.

The way where the imaginary seems real.

The way where getting what you want seems easy.

The way where what is absolute seems undeniably powerful.

The way where representations seem incoherent.

The way where emptiness seems unobtrusive.

The way where what is incoherent can seem meaningless.

The way where what is irrational seems stupid.

The way where perpetual motion seems to be the best area to study.

The way where innocence is usually unexpected.

The way where anything can seem completely new.

---

[1] "Key Work on Pareidolia". Coppedge, N. October 12, 2023

COHERENT-ANTITHEORY

The way where intuition appears impossible.

The way where labeling appears nonsensical.

The way where confusing arguments appear problematic.

The way where certainty appears to provide answers.

The way where metaphors appear to be mesmerizing.

The way where most things seem to appear to be rated average.

The way where calculations appear to confuse you.

The way where advanced yogis sound completely crazy.

The way where what is evolved seems to cheat.

The way where being a kid does not seem important.

The way where complex problems seem to require a simple solution.

COHERENT-DISINTEGRAL

Disintegration seems oddly impossible.

Nonsense seems non-physical.

Relativity seems to cut a Gordian Knot.

Vagrants seem oddly absolute.

There is an odd phenomena where it seems like the sign for 'Aries' is marked on every painting.

There is the odd feeling that a black hole is a singularity.

The way where incoherent things seem to mean something.

The way where irrational things seem especially evil.

The way where there seems to be something uncertain about a paradox.

The way where something naive never seems to be complete.

Coherence and genetics seem oddly similar.

MAGIC-ANTITTHEORY

The way where something new seems antithetical.

The way where verifying is surprising.

The way where problems seem to attract expert advice.

The way where smart rational things seem very stupid.

The way where classification sometimes seems
excessively arbitrary.

The way where measuring things seems a bit average.

The way where mathematics seems incoherent.

The way where thinking something is superhuman
makes it superhuman.

The way where evolution doesn't provide a solution.

The way where reality seems to be somehow trivial.

The way where magic seems too obvious.

ANTITHEORY-DISINTEGRAL

The way where what is ultimately obvious never seems obvious in the beginning.

The way where death matters less to the living.

The way where evolution involves cutting a Gordian Knot.

The way where people who you think cannot survive do survive.

The way where mathematics rarely seems to lead to just one place.

The way where it can be easy to count one thing but hard to count two things.

The way where one example is unhelpful yet two feels too extreme.

The way where cerebralism seems to attract evil geniuses.

The way where what is deeply problematic seems to give us a sixth sense.

The way where we never seem to have knowledge on the most important things.

The way where opposites seem to match.

MODULE: CORRELATIONS *May 21, 2020.*

Greater Correlations, 1

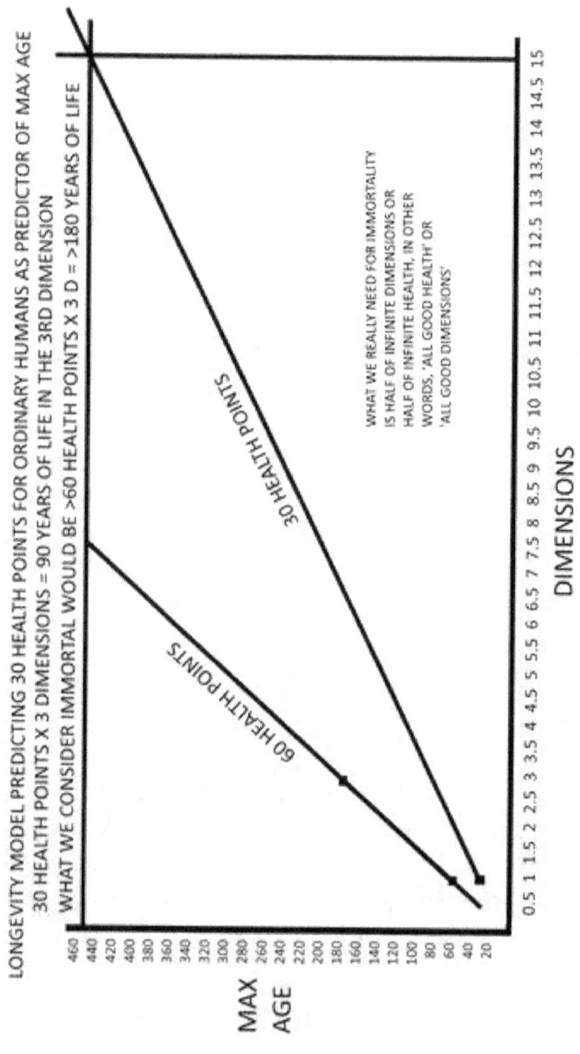

If longevity is always dimensions X health points, this implies dimensions is always spatial dimensions. This is supported by <u>Unique Universe Formulas</u>, where dimensions has been seen to be most accurately depicted as Conceptual Dimensions, which are equivalent to spatial dimensions.

...

OTHER CORRELATIONS:

"The psyche can design design." —The Corollaries

"Strong correlations are also called weird relationships." — <u>Missing Links</u> (...)

According to my Dad, who is a political scientist, causation implies causation, although not really even that, because we HAVE to be reductive. <u>If correlation doesn't imply causation, what does?</u> (...)

An appropriate correlation may imply a particular intelligent type of causation. —<u>Tactile Intelligence</u> (...)

Consciousness-as-Singularity: some events correlated with consciousness. —<u>Mental Wormholes</u> (...)

The concept that any number of arguments apply to a context, because of indefinite correlation. An object is no more than the key to significance, but it has an application for every other object with which it might be correlated. If there are infinite objects, there are many infinities of correlations. —<u>The Subtle Rules of Pseudophysics</u> (...)

The biggest connection I could find is that both pain and taking heavy drugs result in glossy eyes, whereas soulless eyes are created by not staring in the mirror at all, and intense eyes are created by staring in the mirror. Wild eyes are created by fight-or-flight. Glossy eyes also sometimes means sensitivity to drugs or pain.

—<u>Does higher intelligence correlate with brighter or more intense eyes?</u> (...)

Fun serious things are correlated with unserious boredom, and fun-but-not-serious is correlated with serious boredom. —<u>Why is the word "Fun" a subjective term?</u> (...)

Correlation, for example, actionable —<u>Original Categorical Modal Logic</u> (...)

Physical correlation that is not correlated. A succession of arbitrary extras... *Application of the same parts to a more general theory. Correlation ex reductio.* — <u>Binded Logic</u> (...)

Good benefits: correlated with ideas. —<u>So-Called Sketchy Generalism</u> (...)

Direct correlation —<u>What are some of the main arguments in favor of empiricism?</u> (...)

Perception or correlation. Relation, connection. 2-degree relations. —<u>Degree Randomness</u> (...)

It's easier to posit pre-correlation than absoluteness —<u>Rules of Ideas</u> (...)

(If) it is a causal essence to move immediately from the pre-emotional to the absolute, ... it seems that the causal essence is much like emotion. —<u>Emotional Correlation</u> (...)

Correlation between form and emotions —<u>Research on Advanced Ideologies</u> (...)

Certain conditions hold when X and Y correlate. Correlation does not imply inter-causation. —<u>Study of the Inexorable</u> (...)

[Correlation may imply causation?] Take a certain number of effects (efficiencies) which exclusively produce a result, and stated correctly. the (total result - the total efficiency) may produce the sum of relevant differences. Any possible result within the range of efficiencies and differences then represents part of the exclusive cause for the total result. —<u>Pinnacle Theories</u> (...)

Problematic condition leads to a negative correlation of related condition. For example, bad philosophy produces pragmatism where pragmatism opposes philosophy. A means of predicting rules without assuming systematic properties. <u>High-Minded Colundrum</u> (...)

See also:

<u>Accompaniment for Correlative Reasoning and Causal Inference</u> (...)

<u>The Correlation of the Sublimated Heavens</u> (...)

What are the cases in which correlation DOES imply causation?

Philosophically, there are several cases I can think of:

1. **If the effect has an acceptable cause, then the effect is correlated with the cause.**
2. **If, under a particular formalism a behavior is *feasible* (prior-to-effect), then the behavior is correlated under the formalism, subject to empirical enquiry.**
3. **If an effect corresponds ('matches') the data, it is said to be *defeasibly* correlated, that is, after the effect.**
4. **If a cause is correlated with an effect.**

So that is it: FEASIBLE, DEFEASIBLE, ACCEPTABLE, and CAUSAL.

And there is one more which is possible logical correlations.

So, FEASIBLE, DEFEASIBLE, ACCEPTABLE, CAUSAL, and SOMETIMES LOGICAL.

—<u>What are some cases in which correlation does imply causation?</u> (...)

...

Is the correlation *causal* or instead *non-causal* ?

If causal, refer to:

- Syllogisms: <u>15 Valid Forms: Mark McIntire</u> (...)
- Prediction Techniques: <u>Predictive Modeling</u> (...)

If non-causal, refer to coherent systems:

- Coherence: <u>What is categorical deduction?</u> (...)

—<u>How will a machine know that 2 variables are correlated?</u> (...)

...

MISSING LINKS:

IRREPLACEABLE HISTORY

Another theory was the theory of essential cause. If something is truer than something else, it may be the earlier thing of that kind. The more original kind has higher intelligence of the same kind. Therefore, whatever theory is intelligent is the original theory of a kind.

THE 'MISSED STEM'

What happens when ancient divination and cutting-edge technology come together?

I'll try to make a list of the 'obvious' answers:

- It is a 'missed stem' in the interface development hierarchy, so valuable aesthetically and technologically. Magic and divination have an aesthetic that could make the internet more enjoyable and potentially more engaging ('contrapuntal').
- Divination such as psychic prediction techniques could be used to improve the performance of some types of predictions, such as those used for personal divination or personal interfaces. For example, it could result in gamification of the internet, and higher levels of technology.
- There could be increased interest in resource and technology speculation. The interfaces could

increase the fluidity of the economy, and create new business ventures. For example, divination might be something interesting for bank interfaces, or for government-banking systems. Some might call this a slip towards slipperier economics.

- There could also be general implications of combining magic and technology. This may mean for example a new form of 'magic' that is not 'magical' but instead 'technological'. A good example of this is perpetual motion technologies, or coherent magic using luck rays or perpetual motion attributes.

MISSING INFORMATION

BIZARRE THEORIES THAT MIGHT BE RIGHT: NATHAN MIGHT HAVE ENCHANTED BAD LUCK: Picture someone dropping a hot dog with ketchup behind Nathan's chair. Then people gather in small crowds to discuss how it looks gay.

1

Divine anthropology

A virgin, a diamond in the rough…

1.01

Telomeres eat you up and you become an immortal woman. Women are the nature of genetics.

2

WEIRD RELATIONSHIPS

Strong correlations are also called weird relationships. The logic of correlation that I have found is:

LOGIC OF WEIRD RELATIONSHIPS:

FORMULA:

Fancy thing:

Ex: Perpetual motion machines.

(COMPARED WITH)

Substance of 'greater class does':

[For ex, Factories] Plural if possible.

COMBINE FIRST WITH SECOND AS BEST YOU CAN, PLACING THE FIRST FIRST.

This would say 'perpetual motion has a weird relationship with factories'.

So, confounding variables would be anything that contradicts this, or which contradicts a different theory of correlation.

These fall into different classes, but many of them are quantum or weird (not all).

…

PROOF

Fancy thing is something exceptional within a genus. (Ex: Perpetual motion machines).

A content of a genus can always be compared with the genus for similarity, as it shares some characteristic.

Therefore, we can say 'compares with' = relationship.

If the comparison is determined as a function of the fancy thing, e.g. what the fancy thing 'does' (no matter whether 'does' is empty or not), we can see 'does' as having a correlation with the genus at least tentatively, because the genus has at least a passing similarity to the fancy thing, and thus can be classed at least superficially as either doing something similar to being related to the same class.

This is less true if the 'larger class does' is not the true class of the fancy thing, thus, the correlation becomes empirically verifiable to some degree, completing the basic requirements for correlation. ('Does' covers some of the causal component, as 'does' implies some sort of cause-effect response with the environment which is implied to be related to the 'larger class does').

A more general simplification might be 'the action of the function is related to the class of the function.'

...

Further Examples:

The weird correspondence between infinity and eyesight.

The weird correspondence between parents wanting to lose weight and their kids developing depression.

The exhuberant relationship between free will, purpose, and fakes (e.g. if 13 dimensions seems appropriate, it may be because it is not the right number: if it is not the right number it seems to be fake, which gives the impression of its being under human control, which in turn endows it with artificial purpose).

The weird relationship between significance and quantum relationships.

The weird relationship between intelligent animals and perversity.

The weird relationship between understanding metaphors and hurting children.

The weird relationship between armor crafting and true genius.

The weird alternative-associativistic yet causal relationship of dinosaurs and the undead.

The weird quantum relationship of psychopathy and perpetual motion and God.

The weird quantum relationship of mud and blood.

The weird quantum relationship of animals and black holes.

The weird magnetic relationship of invention and contusity.

The weird academic relationship of magic and essence.

The weird associative relationship of immortals and vampires.

The weird uncanny correspondence relationship of telepathy and death.

The uncanny link between the word 'quasi' and the word 'crazy'.

The probable causal relationship between 'rating something premier' (cause) and 'human being' (effect).

The weird automatic relationship between monadic health and the death of the universe.

The weird automatic relationship between archemechanical health and death machines.

The weird fast correspondence relationship between magic swords and magic death.

The weird exclusive relationship between perpetual motion and factories.

The quantum equality of the visionary and science institutions in regards to the overmind.

The quantum relationship between perfectionism and mild depression.

The weird entangled relationship between intellectualism and schizophrenia.

The weird physical relationship between mosquitos and elephants heads.

The strange compensatory relationship between social responsibility and personal sanity.

The weird fiscal relationship between generalism and irrelevance.

The transcriptive relationship between tilting and sublime complexity and horizontal rotation and sublime complexity.

The weird correlation between coffee and a brain damaged society.

The weird inverse correlation between people played false and people branded fake.

The horrible coincidence of the presence of maggots and meaningless repetition.

The odd compulsory relationship between feelings of disgust and things that are worthwhile.

The incidental pairing between the word 'slopped' and the word 'slept'.

The auspicious relationship of keys and raising the dead.

The diabolical relationship between curtsying and curses.

The causal relationship between daydreams and nightmares.

The uncanny similarity between anyone's else's born enemies and bohemians.

The morbid relationship between <u>Windfalls</u> and <u>Angel Studies</u>

The weird subtle relationship between revenge and mutants or anti-mutes who were once mutes.

The uncanny relationship between sublime constants and a failed divorce.

The uncanny relationship between sleepwalking and driving.

The uncanny relationship between peacefulness and gamblers.

The uncanny relationship between bad ethics and the concept of eternal return.

The causal relationship between creating djinns and becoming slaves.

The automatic relation between pantomimes and slave-traders.

The weird involvement between mortality and magic walls [consult Einstein's relatives].

The unusual relationship between double-negation and gaining weight.

The odd compulsion between activity and culture.

The strong connection between loyalty and responsibility.

The weird familiarity between magic and life.

The weird seeming of reasoning and the macabre.

The maddening relationship between the appearance of clones and the ability to time-travel.

The haunting relationship between soullessness and exploring spooky places

WRONG CONCEPTS

The view that Hegel is the 'first ironist'. On the face of it, it sounds like sort of the wrong concept. Assuming it's wrong, let's continue...

Here are similar instances:

- Emily Dickinson's Inanimus should have been the Simulagra.
- The sci-fi writing on 'the simulator' should have been 'the emulator'.
- Theodore Roethke's 'all accented line' should have been 'over-unity language'.
- The theory on high stress should have been a theory of some type of fatigue.
- Benjamin Franklin's lightning rod should have been 'energy architecture'.
- Amadeus Mozart's symphonic method maybe should have been 'emotional architecture'.
- Francis Galton's supremecism concept should have been the same as 'superiority', unless he can prove being 'supreme' is any better than being 'superior'.
- Nietzsche's uber-mensche should have just been superhumanism unless they

can make big boobs work for a lot of
people.

- The view that Hegel is the 'first ironist'.
  It should have been the 'last ironist'
  because they didn't own their weapons
  after that.
- The view that Twain is the 'first futurist'.
  It should have been 'the most lazy
  futurist' because he's Mark Twain. —
  Wrong Concepts

...

Mental Superstrategies

Hell: NEGATIVE DIMENSIONS
Jinxes, Monsters: NIRVANA
Air conditioning, Tarot: TOOLS
The Fortunate Man: THEORY
Economics, Prostitutes: EVOLUTION
Time-Travel: LOOPS
Disguisery: WEAKNESS
Military Snipers: NINJAS
Burger, Ketchup, Cartoons: INDIVIDUAL
Introverts, Metaphysics: UNIQUES
Perfect Childhood: LANGUAGE
Lucifer: INTERNET
The Calculus: APPLICATIONS
Generalism: MEANING
Genocide: SURVIVAL
Photography, Imagination: CORES
Heavy Hormones: DRUGS
Computers, Interfaces: MATH
Occult, Genius: SKILL
Philosophy, Perpetual Motion: POWER
Applied Perpetual Motion: COMPLEXITY

Knowledge of matter can lead somewhere good (… for the soul)… Knowledge of the soul can lead somewhere bad (… for the soul)… Freedom for the soul might lead somewhere good for pure matter or lower dimensions, whereas freedom of matter might lead somewhere good for the pure soul or higher dimensions. —<u>Source</u>

Integrations:

Dimensions: Good architecture is a miracle pill.

Behavior: Complex lexicon.

Immortality: Nifty forest.

Coherence: We need a new equation.

Events: Weather. Lightning flashes.

Linguistics: The logic of losing Coleridge's diaries.

Language and Earwax: The soul.

Money: Metal objects.

Physics: Radioactive ice water.

Soul: That bathroom is a nightmare made for dinosaurs.

Spells: The end is only the beginning.

Utopia: God is a parasite.

—<u>Quintessential Ideas Experimental</u>

Pseudo Equations:

If God is a cannibal, something is not human.

Subjective Nirvana: They're just being skeptical & similar.

The secret of Hell is, its empty and it hurts.

Technological children = fatherhood + coincidence and serendipity.

Elitism: It's just elitism isn't it = IDK.

See what is charged for stupidity? Everything, apparently not including stupidity.

Satan is a representation of authentic bias.

Second third infinity of fallacies is what many multiple correspondence relies on, as correspondence is potentially a fallacy which compounds with number of correspondences.

Fortune: Things change when its no big deal.

Depression: Overthinking how to underthink.

Everything about China is prophetic to Lao. If Lao is immortal he will be shackled.

Fashionable: Two minutes of God's time.

Cheaper People: They are more authentic, because they have more freedom or less history.

Fantasy and the coincidence of how you treat everyone: the damage to souls.

What do we trust except authenticity, so you shouldn't assume I'm the one causing the problems.

There's always a complex explanation that works, when lies are involved.

If God has you by the p****, you might think you're God.

It seems if someone wants to send me to hell, life must seem too good to them, they think something is wrong with life and living.

Cubists invented ghosts. The greatest Cubist invented the greatest ghost.

It's madness if it's impractical.

Animistic mind: Irrational personality in a very sane setting.

Let's consider that my complaint could be of weight. True, my (complaint) may have token value. In the information age, token value was played bigtime.

Token value may be relevant. Therefore, my complaint may be relevant. Where my complaint may be relevant, you should take my complaint as though it were serious. If that is the case, what does it mean if my complaint is of weight? It could be very weighty indeed!

If we know our aggression we transcend.

If something is really fun to say, you might not care what the truth is.

Ambiguity about irrationality is just sane people messing up.

How to lie like Lucipher: Be honest.

Gods are always-happy people who somehow understand pain.

You see people similar to you no matter what you look like, unless you're an authentic person or a crazy person. Normal people always want to be authentic people. Crazy people think maybe they want to be authentic people. Authentic people are envious of crazy people. Crazy people are envious of authentic people.

Parfit's Formula for Becoming Lucifer: Parfit says either the soul or ideas is real, and we should do something with that (if we can, if we know what to do, unless it has bad consequences).

Thoughts humans smother to death: Sounds violent but it feels soft.

Social karma from talking out loud creates schizophrenic voices.

Unavoidable Survival Principle: One of my guesses is that those who are very rare, but do not find their existence valuable tend to be very tough human beings who have more life left to live. The principle of how consciousness avoids unnecessary experiences.

Emptiness is the death of monism.

Shower thoughts: The more productive you are relative to your intelligence, the less you will have shower thoughts, by a fixed quantity, rather than a fraction of the total.

Caucasian women that are not uninteresting are trappists, or the world is going crazy, or Nathan Coppedge is the world.

An alternate symbol can involve less responsibility.

Values can be successful fakes unless you have an absolute advantage.

Rational philosophy leaves ridiculousness about two absolute degrees behind.

—<u>The Pseudo Equations</u> (…)

Quantum idiocy --> weird flash.

Reincarnation --> Immortality secret.

Elemental ruminance --> pleasant games.

Bird tree fish language --> bad luck power.

Options --> psychic scenarios.

Exaggeration --> Telekinesis.

Consumer --> Over-Under

Nature --> Organon

FURTHER:

Head, something to fight for → Bull, Horns. Had general thoughts.

Children, vulnerability → Ducks, ducklings. Was innocent about children.

Thought, baseness → Chimpanzee, being tricked. Jumped ahead.

Wonder, lost → Exotic bird, imagery. Has images.

Swan, figure → Voluptuous, belief in animals. Has a concept of form.

Dog, holes → Dog, burying things in holes. God was all.

Scratching, hair → Show horse, escapade = escapa / escapad. Wrong education.

Popular, defense → Birds, differences. Defending popular opinions.

Say:

Head, something to fight for → Bull, Horns. Had general thoughts.

Children, vulnerability → Ducks, ducklings. Was innocent about children.

Thought, baseness → Chimpanzee, being tricked. Jumped ahead.

Wonder, lost → Exotic bird, imagery. Has images.

Swan, figure → Voluptuous, belief in animals. Has a concept of form.

Dog, holes → Dog, burying things in holes. God was all.

Scratching, hair → Show horse, escapade = escapa / escapad. Wrong education.

Popular, defense → Birds, differences. Defending popular opinions. —<u>Logic of Spirit Animals</u>

MEDICAL:

The mutually exclusive relationship of sleeping and blood circulation.

…

Difficult pebbles.

Difficult problems.

Manageable walking.

Suddenly swimming.

Alternately flying.

Emotional weather.

Token objects.

Sublime machines.

Orgasming systems.

Epiphanical reality.

Impossible impossibility.

Problematic problems.

Real virtue.

Virtual realism.

Paradigmatic paradoxes.

Degrees of absoluteness.

Supreme exotericism.

Subtle physics.

Obsolete medicines.

Emperor's chop-mark.

Magical moods.

Singular consciousness.

Glimpse of eternity.

Tolerant reality.

Philosophical problems.

Sublime terror.

—<u>Sublime Metaphysics: Moody Mudra</u>

CHOICE DILEMMAS:

Metaphysics and Wholesome and meaningful life

Design and Greatness

BASED ON THE PREMIER INTELLECTUAL DIALECTIC, A COMPLETE OR UNFINISHED SET OF 2-STEPS:

ENERGY 2-STEPS:

→ Arcadian Apparata (Divine Beauty), Stygian Automata (Diabolical Genius)

→ Compati-Volition, aims to find similarities between different models (Modular Set Volition), Standard Volition, aims to standardize energy computation depending on the characteristics of a specific model (Singular Cycle Volition)

→ Natural Torque (Varying-Altitude Wave Volition), Natural Momentum (Varying Altitude-Speed Volition)

→ Coincidental Motion (Integrated Volitional Mechanics), Volitional Momentum (Resulting Perpetual Motion)

→ Real Windows (Ingenious Ratios), Impossible Magic (Near-Magical Behavior)

→ Volitional Equations (Volitional Universal Constants), Volitional Energy (Volitional Variable Constants)

→ Ubiquitous Mobility (Constant Haptic Volition), Mobile Channels (Haptic Transfer Volition)

→ Rube Goldberg Pieces (Volitional Objects), Immortal Aesthetic (Perpetual Landscapes)

→ Conducion, meaning hyper-compatible energy systems, including Volitional Actuator 'leap-wire' (Volitional Conductive Activity), Exponential Energy (Activity of Volitional Production)

→ Master Angle (Higher Eccentric Recovery), Vescension / Devescension (Higher Volitional Recovery)

MAGIC 2-STEPS:

→ Soul (Precaution of Premature Magic), God (Precaution of Masterful Mastery)

→ Wish-Blessings (Magical Essence), Immortality (Magical Vitality)

→ Spells-Enchantments (Natural Magic), Magical Character (Magical Nature)

→ Enchanted Memory (Memory), Enchanted Warding (Warding)

→ Summon an Evil Element(Do Harm), Summon a Good Element (Do Good)

→ Possess Person (Magical Control), Charm Person (Magical Charm)

→ Fortitude (Magical Strength), InveighanceInculcation-Circle-of-Protection (General Spiritual Protection)

→ Magical Channeling (Magical Power Channels), The Power (Metaphysical Power)

→ The Sorceror (Wild Natures), The Psychical (Subtle Natures)

→ Wizardry (Magic-at-Will), Satrapy (Knowledge-at-Will)

PHILOSOPHY 2-STEPS:

→ The Meaning of Life (Existential Meaning), Philosophy (Existential Anxiety)

→ Perception (Existential Awareness), Transcendence (Metaphysical Awareness)

→ Knowledge of Absolutes (Absolute Knowledge), Psychology (Qualified Knowledge)

→ Character (Humility), Greatness (Aspiration)

→ Extremity (Madness), Neutrality (Reasonableness)

→ Paradoxical Paradoxes (Solving Paradoxes), The Problem of Evil (Having Trouble)

→ Justice (Weighing the Good), Contradiction (Weighing the Bad)

→ Illumination (Justified Awareness), Consciousness (Awareness Insight)

→ Complexity (Rational Ideas), Incompleteness (Irrational Ideas)

→ Patience (Adequate Uncertainty), Satisfaction (Adequate Pleasure)

MATH 2-STEPS:

→ Power (Factor Decideratum), Equation (Emergence Decideratum)

→ Desirability (Property Paradigms), Advantageousness (Efficient Properties)

Science… To include Advanced … Math… (Harmonious)… One perhaps related perspective is that of Logic… Higher translation in terms of (Similar, Multiple) Logic… Logic ingeniously to arrive at Harmonious Compatibility. Harmonious Compatibility can be used for Similar Harmonies and Group Harmonies.

→ Law of Identity (Logic of Similar Harmonies), Law of Proportion (Logic of Group Harmonies)

→ The Supernatural (Magical Results), The Natural (Consequential Results)

→ Law of Inherency (Unlimited Compatible Logic), Law of Correlation (Limited Compatible Logic)

→ Mathematical Trickery (Informal Enculcation), Mathematical Law (Formal Enculcation)

→ Mathematical Derivatives (Derivative Logic), Mathematical Integrals (Integrated Logic)

→ Material Forms (Applied Forms), Universals (Container Forms)

→ Law of Sufficiency (Mathematical Sufficiency), Law of Sequences (Mathematical Succession)

→ Law of Joined Identicals (Determinism by Theoretical Compatibility), Law of Complete Completeness (Determinism by Proof Compatibility)

MISC 2-STEPS:

(High Anachronysms, Dimensional Seasons)

(Omni-Sense, Anything Theory)

(Transcend Essence, Essential Transcendence)

(Wisteria, Magical Wishes)

(Soul Searching Principle, Wish Fulfillment Symbol)

(Unbelievable Success, Radical Average)

(Primary Ideas, Secondary Ideas)

(Money Products, Lucky Inventions)

(Regenerative Mechanism, Defensive Mechanism)

MINOR WEIRD RELATIONS (Noticed Nov 1, 2020 from an earlier document dated April 10, 2020):

Intuition from apparent contradiction.

Beauty from ugliness.

Superficial danger.

Strange anomalies.

Exceptional knowledge.

Paradigms on the verge of obliteration.

Nodes: projects.

Branches: comprehending.

Speed: processing speed.

Range: connected with social acceptance.

Tokens: meditations.

Views: visages.

Identity: sublime.

Solomon: poles, metaphysics.

Whoever throws an apple core is a poet.

Whoever sees half a bridge is sexy.

Whoever sees that the universe is an infinite apple core is a time-traveler.

Whoever is God in heaven is making magical soup.

Gelatin recipes: Science and cooking.

Optical illusions: Art and psychology.

Board games: Design and psychology.

Toys: Invention and aesthetics.

Computer games: Computers and storytelling.

Perpetual motion machines: Philosophy and engineering.

Easier to communicate with ideas when you're dead.

A gay person cursed with straight becomes a pedophile.

A straight person cursed with gay becomes a schizophrenic.

More Possible Weird Relationships in an Earlier Attempt to be Coherent, finally Located:

Priorities:

Black Swan History

Sublime Interface

Anachronistic Transport

Archetypal Mechanics

Nothing without Nothing (= within)

Special Numbers

Coherent Iterations

Ideal Categories

Perfect Systems

Fast Connections

Lucky Anomalies

Divine Symbols

Self-solving Puzzles

Big Words

Wonderful Ideas

Dynamic World

Vacant Traps

Artificial Decay

—<u>Premier Thought Studies 3</u>

New + Modern.

Captivation + Enchantment.

Forms + Functions.

Matter + Myth.

Fun + Adventure.

Great + Small.

Sensuous + Mysterious.

Dark + Meaningful.

Arranged + Proud.

Fine + Gleaming.

Strong + Worthy.

Strange + Bold.

Rich + Deserved.

Implacable + Forthright.

Wild + Hysterical.

Soulful + Significant.

Just + Good. —<u>Catalog of Synthesis</u>

TRIREMES

Clothes on Shoes Nasty = Consciousness?

Bird = But absurd?

Mink = Missing link?

Trireme = Tired dream?

CORRELATIONS AND EXCLUSIVE LISTS

- A correlation is likely to have a 'type' of cause in a 1:1 correlation which is the type of correlation.
- Another case is if there is a 1:1 correlation between exclusive sets. In this case, there is one cause, but the correlation occurs between exclusive sets. In this case the type of cause is still the type of correlation.

MISC

Pronounced Loudly On Heaven:

Insect heaven is the sky. The air supports them as they smell stuff.

Dog heaven is the basement. So many odds and ends to chew on.

Human heaven is an alcove where they can read and talk.

Mut-ube attracts anti-mutes who were once mutes.

CONNECTION BETWEEN HEROES AND PEACE

On the topic of heroes, I have noted that successful heroes tend to be approaches to abandoning war:

1. Inventing war, e.g. war as a solution to an underlying conflict.

2. Evil bargain, e.g. attempt to save a race from higher wrath.

3. A philosopher who dreams dangerous dreams like perpetual motion machines.

4. Great responsibility, for example, a religious leader that causes her people to do evil deeds.

5. A trickster who gets into a lot of trouble, like hurting someone to help someone.

6. Astonishing Wonders, for example, the cure for Cancer.

7. Change of mentality, for example, an optimistic leader.

8. Creating unity in society.

9. Initiator into a time of peace.

10. Causing return to simple ways.

11. Destroying the species.

—How do you feel about war, what could be an alternative, or is there no alternative?

...

See also: Alternate Education 101 (personalities arranged like super-strategies)

OBLIQUE ETHICS

Oblique = obligé.

Battles are bad, bottles are good.

If myth is bad math is good, doesn't that mean bad myth?

Females are bad, feline companions are good.

Ferrous is bad, ferris wheels are made of stainless steel.

People are bad, popular is good.

Banks are bad, buttons are good.

Whelks are bad, rogues / Romans / robes are good.

History is bad, hysteria is good.

Elite is bad, chrome is good.

Potash is bad, ruminating is good.

Feasts are bad, religious sanctimony is good.

Zits are bad, zit cream is good.

Feistiness is good, policy and policing is bad.

Hysteria is good, the Hanged Man is bad.

Recourse is good, reasoning / recollection is bad.

,,,

BIO

Nathan Coppedge or Nathan Larkin Coppedge (b.1982) , is a philosopher, artist, inventor, poet, and member of the international honor society for philosophers. A prolific author with over 200 books published on Amazon, he is a perpetual motioneer, famous quotable, and internationally-selling Hyper-Cubist. A one-time member of Tesla Society UK online and PESWiki, and founder of many Facebook groups, he lives near Yale University.

www.ingramcontent.com/pod-product-compliance
Lightning Source LLC
Chambersburg PA
CBHW071217260726
48653CB00041B/892